CISA

Cheat Sheet

1st Edition

VERSAtile Reads

Chapter 01: Secrets of a Successful Auditor

Understanding the Demand for IS Audits: Explores why audits are crucial for information systems, driven by regulatory demands and corporate accountability.

Executive Misconduct: *Covers the role of IS audits in detecting and preventing executive-level fraud or unethical practices.*

More Regulation Ahead: *Highlights the increasing regulatory landscape and its impact on audit requirements.*

Basic Regulatory Objective: *The core goal of regulations is to protect stakeholders by ensuring transparency, accountability, and integrity.*

Governance Is Leadership: *Defines governance as leading and directing to ensure organizational objectives are met.*

Three Types of Data Target Different Uses [1.1]: *Data is categorized into types, each serving specific purposes like decision-making, compliance, or operational needs.*

Audit Results Indicate the Truth: *Audit findings reveal factual data about system performance, compliance, and effectiveness.*

Understanding Policies, Standards, Guidelines, and Procedures [1.2]: Differentiates these foundational documents, which guide and regulate organizational operations and audits.

Understanding Professional Ethics: Defines ethical guidelines that professionals, particularly auditors, must follow.

Following the ISACA Professional Code: *Explains adherence to ISACA's ethics code, essential for IS auditors.*

Preventing Ethical Conflicts: *Guidance on avoiding conflicts of interest, ensuring objective audits.*

Understanding the Purpose of an Audit: The core aim of audits is to assess and verify compliance, integrity, and performance of systems.

Classifying General Types of Audits: *Identifies various audit types (financial, operational, compliance) and their purposes.*

Determining Differences in Audit Approach: *Audits vary in approach depending on scope, focus, and objectives.*

Understanding the Auditor's Responsibility: *Outlines an auditor's duties to ensure impartial and accurate findings.*

Comparing Audits to Assessments: *Differences between audits (formal, compliance-focused) and assessments (often informal, improvement-focused).*

Differentiating between Auditor and Auditee Roles: Defines roles: auditors conduct reviews; auditees are those being audited.

Applying an Independence Test: *Ensures auditors remain unbiased and independent from the organization they audit.*

Implementing Audit Standards: The application of standards to ensure audits are consistent, fair, and reliable.

Where Do Audit Standards Come From? *Audit standards are established by professional bodies like ISACA, ensuring best practices.*

Understanding the Various Auditing Standards: *Detailed audit standards for quality, ethics, and procedural consistency.*

Specific Regulations Defining Best Practices: *Certain regulations outline best practices that guide audit quality and methodology.*

Audits to Prove Financial Integrity: *Financial audits ensure accurate, transparent reporting of an organization's finances.*

Auditor Is an Executive Position: Auditors hold high-ranking roles with significant influence over audit processes and outcomes.

Understanding the Importance of Auditor Confidentiality: *Confidentiality is critical to protect sensitive information uncovered during audits.*

Working with Lawyers: *Collaboration with legal teams to ensure audits meet regulatory and legal standards.*

Working with Executives: *Engaging with executives to understand strategic objectives and areas of concern.*

Working with IT Professionals: *Interacting with IT teams to validate technical aspects of systems under audit.*

Retaining Audit Documentation: *Documenting findings thoroughly to provide a record of the audit process and outcomes.*

Providing Good Communication and Integration: *Ensuring clear communication between auditors and other stakeholders for a cohesive audit process.*

Understanding Leadership Duties: *Auditors in leadership roles plan, oversee, and execute audit tasks and team management.*

Planning and Setting Priorities: *Determining audit priorities based on risk assessment and organizational goals.*

Providing Standard Terms of Reference: *Setting clear objectives* and scope to guide the audit process effectively.

Dealing with Conflicts and Failures: *Approaches for managing disputes and handling situations when audits reveal major issues.*

Identifying the Value of Internal and External Auditors: *Internal auditors offer ongoing insight, while external auditors provide independent verification.*

Understanding the Evidence Rule: *Evidence gathered in audits must be sufficient, reliable, and verifiable.*

Stakeholders: Identifying Whom You Need to Interview: *Determining key stakeholders to interview for comprehensive audit insights.*

Understanding the Corporate Organizational Structure: Knowing the hierarchy and structure helps auditors identify audit impacts and responsibilities.

Identifying Roles in a Corporate Organizational Structure [1.3]: Recognizes different corporate roles (e.g., executives, managers) relevant to the audit.

Identifying Roles in a Consulting Firm Organizational Structure [1.4]: Defines roles in consulting firms, including auditors and supporting consultants.

Chapter 02: Governance

Strategy Planning for Organizational Control [2.1]: Involves setting policies and plans to guide organizational behavior and maintain control over processes.

Overview of the IT Steering Committee [2.2]: A group that guides IT-related decisions and aligns IT strategy with business goals.

Using the Balanced Scorecard (BSC): A tool for tracking and managing organizational performance across financial, customer, internal, and learning metrics.

IT Subset of the BSC: Customizing the Balanced Scorecard specifically for IT, focusing on technology's role in organizational success.

Decoding the IT Strategy: Understanding how IT strategy supports broader business objectives and addresses competitive needs.

Specifying a Policy: Establishing specific rules and guidelines to direct organizational and IT-related actions.

Project Management: Processes for planning, executing, and overseeing projects to achieve specific organizational goals.

Implementation Planning of the IT Strategy [2.3]: Detailed planning of how to execute and realize the IT strategy effectively within the organization.

Using COBIT: COBIT is a framework for managing and governing enterprise IT, aligning IT processes with business objectives.

Identifying Sourcing Locations: Choosing internal or external sources for IT functions based on cost, skill, and strategic alignment.

Conducting an Executive Performance Review: Evaluating executive contributions to ensure alignment with strategic and operational objectives.

Understanding the Auditor's Interest in the Strategy: Auditors review strategic alignment to ensure it meets compliance, risk, and organizational goals.

Overview of Tactical Management: Day-to-day management of resources and activities to achieve immediate organizational objectives.

Planning and Performance: Involves setting short-term goals and measuring performance to ensure alignment with organizational strategy.

Management Control Methods: Techniques like budgeting, variance analysis, and key performance indicators (KPIs) to monitor organizational activities.

Risk Management: Identifying, assessing, and mitigating risks to protect organizational assets and operations.

Implementing Standards: Applying industry and regulatory standards to ensure quality, security, and compliance in operations.

Human Resources: Managing workforce requirements to support organizational needs, including hiring, training, and development.

System Life-Cycle Management: Overseeing the entire life cycle of IT systems, from inception to disposal, ensuring relevance and performance.

Continuity Planning: Preparing for business continuity in the face of disruptions to maintain essential functions.

Insurance: Financial protection against risks to help organizations recover from potential losses.

Overview of Business Process Reengineering (BPR): Redesigning business processes for major performance improvements in areas like efficiency and quality.

Why Use Business Process Reengineering: To achieve significant gains by fundamentally rethinking how tasks are performed.

BPR Methodology: Structured approaches to identifying, analyzing, and redesigning processes for better outcomes.

Genius or Insanity? The debate over BPR's effectiveness can be transformative or challenging depending on execution.

The goal of BPR: is to achieve significant improvements in cost, quality, service, and speed.

Guiding Principles for BPR: Fundamental principles such as focusing on customer needs and prioritizing value creation.

Knowledge Requirements for BPR: Understanding technical and organizational factors that impact the redesign process.

BPR Techniques: Tools and methods, like process mapping and flow analysis, are used to streamline operations.

BPR Application Steps: The steps for applying BPR, from identifying needs to evaluating redesigned processes.

Role of IS in BPR: Information systems are crucial in BPR for automating processes and supporting redesigns.

Business Process Documentation: Detailed documentation of current processes to aid in analysis and redesign.

BPR Data Management Techniques: *Methods to collect, store, and analyze data efficiently for process improvements.*

Benchmarking as a BPR Tool: *Using industry benchmarks to set performance standards and goals for redesigned processes.*

Using a Business Impact Analysis: *Identifying potential impacts of process changes on the organization's objectives and performance.*

BPR Project Risk Assessment: *Evaluating risks associated with BPR projects to anticipate and mitigate challenges.*

Practical Application of BPR: *Real-world implementation strategies for successful BPR initiatives.*

Practical Selection Methods for BPR: *Criteria and techniques to choose the right processes for reengineering.*

Troubleshooting BPR Problems: *Identifying and solving common challenges in BPR projects.*

Understanding the Auditor's Interest in Tactical Management: *Auditors focus on tactical management to ensure daily activities align with organizational control and goals.*

Operations Management: Managing day-to-day operations to ensure efficiency and alignment with strategic objectives.

Sustaining Operations: *Ensuring continuous and stable operations through adequate resources and management.*

Tracking Actual Performance: *Monitoring performance against set targets to identify areas for improvement.*

Controlling Change: *Managing and controlling changes to maintain stability and compliance in operational activities.*

Understanding the Auditor's Interest in Operational Delivery: *Auditors review operational delivery to ensure compliance with policies and the effectiveness of controls.*

Chapter 03: Audit Process

Understanding the Audit Program: An organized, systematic approach for conducting audits to ensure compliance and effectiveness.

>   ***Audit Program Objectives and Scope:*** *Defines the purpose and boundaries of the audit to align with organizational goals.*
>
>   ***Audit Program Extent:*** *Determines the depth and breadth of audit activities based on risk and resource availability.*
>
>   ***Audit Program Responsibilities:*** *Outlines roles and duties of individuals involved in the audit program.*
>
>   ***Audit Program Resources:*** *Resources, such as time, budget, and personnel, are required to execute an audit effectively.*
>
>   ***Audit Program Procedures:*** *The steps and methods used to perform the audit, ensuring consistency and thoroughness.*
>
>   ***Audit Program Implementation:*** *Putting the audit program into action, following planned procedures and timelines.*
>
>   ***Audit Program Records:*** *Documentation of all audit activities, providing a clear audit trail.*
>
>   ***Audit Program Monitoring and Review:*** *Continuous oversight and evaluation of the audit program for improvement.*
>
>   *Planning Individual Audits [3.1]: Detailed planning for specific audits tailored to individual objectives and risks.*

Establishing and Approving an Audit Charter: A formal document that authorizes the audit, outlining its scope, objectives, and authority.

>   **Role of the Audit Committee:** *The audit committee oversees the audit process, ensuring it aligns with organizational policies.*

Preplanning Specific Audits: Initial preparations, including gathering background information and setting objectives.

>   ***Understanding the Variety of Audits:*** *Different types of audits (e.g., financial, compliance, IT) serve distinct purposes.*
>
>   *Identifying Restrictions on Scope [3.2]: Limits that affect what can be reviewed within an audit, such as time, resources, or access.*
>
>   ***Gathering Detailed Audit Requirements:*** *Collecting necessary information to define audit focus, objectives, and criteria.*
>
>   ***Using a Systematic Approach to Planning:*** *Following a structured process to organize and conduct audits efficiently.*
>
>   ***Comparing Traditional Audits to Assessments and Self-Assessments:*** *Differences in scope and approach between traditional audits, assessments, and self-assessments.*

Performing an Audit Risk Assessment: Identifying and evaluating risks to determine audit focus and allocate resources.

Determining Whether an Audit Is Possible: Assessing feasibility based on scope, access, and organizational readiness.

>   *Identifying the Risk Management Strategy [3.3]: Audit includes reviewing how an organization manages and mitigates risks.*
>
>   ***Determining Feasibility of Audit:*** *Evaluating whether an audit can be completed given available resources and constraints.*

Performing the Audit: Executing the audit plan involving data collection, testing, and evidence gathering.

>   ***Selecting the Audit Team:*** *Choosing auditors with the right skills and experience for the specific audit.*
>
>   ***Determining Competence and Evaluating Auditors:*** *Assessing auditors' qualifications and performance to ensure audit quality.*
>
>   ***Ensuring Audit Quality Control:*** *Maintaining high standards through oversight and review during the audit process.*
>
>   ***Establishing Contact with the Auditee:*** *Engaging with the Auditee to clarify the audit process and expectations.*
>
>   ***Making Initial Contact with the Auditee:*** *The first interaction to introduce the audit team and outline the audit approach.*
>
>   ***Using Data Collection Techniques:*** *Applying methods like interviews, surveys, and document reviews to gather information.*
>
>   ***Conducting Document Review:*** *Examining relevant documents to verify information and assess controls.*
>
>   ***Understanding the Hierarchy of Internal Controls:*** *Identifying different levels of controls within an organization, from preventive to detective.*
>
>   ***Reviewing Existing Controls:*** *Assessing current controls to ensure they are adequate and functioning properly.*
>
>   ***Preparing the Audit Plan:*** *Creating a detailed audit roadmap, including scope, procedures, and timelines.*
>
>   ***Assigning Work to the Audit Team:*** *Allocating tasks to team*

members based on their expertise and workload.

Preparing Working Documents: *Organizing documents required to conduct and support the audit process.*

Conducting Onsite Audit Activities: *Performing audit tasks on-site, including observations and direct inquiries.*

Gathering Audit Evidence: Collecting data and documentation to support audit findings.

Using Evidence to Prove a Point: *Using gathered evidence to validate findings and conclusions.*

Understanding Types of Evidence: *Various forms of evidence (e.g., physical, documentary, testimonial) are used in audits.*

Selecting Audit Samples: *Choosing representative samples for testing to conclude a population.*

Recognizing Typical Evidence for IS Audits: *Common evidence in information systems audits, like logs, reports, and configurations.*

Using Computer-Assisted Audit Tools: *Software tools to assist in data analysis and testing within an audit.*

Understanding Electronic Discovery: *Process of retrieving and analyzing digital information for audits or investigations.*

Grading of Evidence: *Classifying evidence based on its reliability and relevance.*

Timing of Evidence: *Ensuring evidence is collected within an appropriate timeframe to remain relevant.*

Following the Evidence Life Cycle [3.4]: Managing evidence from collection through storage to final disposition.

Conducting Audit Evidence Testing: Testing collected evidence to verify accuracy and compliance.

Compliance Testing: *Assessing whether controls meet regulatory and organizational requirements.*

Substantive Testing: *Directly verifying data or transactions to confirm completeness and accuracy.*

Tolerable Error Rate: *The acceptable level of error within audit tests, varying by audit scope and objectives.*

Recording Test Results: *Documenting outcomes of tests for use in audit reporting.*

Generating Audit Findings: Compiling results of tests and observations into actionable findings.

Detecting Irregularities and Illegal Acts: *Identifying any fraudulent or non-compliant activities during an audit.*

Indicators of Illegal or Irregular Activity: *Signs of fraud or violations, such as unusual transactions or conflicts of interest.*

Responding to Irregular or Illegal Activity: *Actions to address and report findings of misconduct or irregularities.*

Findings Outside of Audit Scope: *Handling discoveries unrelated to the audit objectives or scope.*

Report Findings: Summarizing and presenting audit results to stakeholders in a final report.

Approving and Distributing the Audit Report: *Ensuring the audit report is reviewed, approved, and shared with appropriate parties.*

Identifying Omitted Procedures: *Recognizing any missed procedures and addressing them as necessary.*

Conducting Follow-up (Closing Meeting): Reviewing findings and discussing the next steps with the auditee to close the audit.

Chapter 04: Networking Technology Basics

Networking Technology Basics: Fundamental concepts of networking, covering key elements such as network types, components, and protocols.

Understanding the Differences in Computer Architecture [4.1]: Examines different computer architectures (e.g., x86, ARM) and their impact on performance and compatibility.

Selecting the Best System: Guidelines for choosing a computer system based on requirements and compatibility with software and hardware.

> *Identifying Various Operating Systems: Overview of popular operating systems (e.g., Windows, Linux, macOS) and their unique features.*

> *Determining the Best Computer Class: Factors to consider when selecting computer classes (e.g., desktop, server, mobile) based on usage needs.*

> *Comparing Computer Capabilities: Comparison of different systems' performance metrics such as processing power, memory, and storage.*

> *Ensuring System Control: Techniques to maintain control over computer systems, including access control and system management.*

> *Dealing with Data Storage [4.2]: Overview of data storage solutions (e.g., HDD, SSD, cloud storage) and data management practices.*

> *Using Interfaces and Ports: Understanding common interfaces and ports (e.g., USB, HDMI, Ethernet) for connecting devices.*

Introducing the Open Systems Interconnection (OSI) Model: A framework for network communication divided into seven layers, each with specific functions.

> *Layer 1: Physical Layer: Manages hardware transmission (e.g., cables, switches).*

> *Layer 2: Data-Link Layer: Establishes direct node-to-node data transfer.*

> *Layer 3: Network Layer: Manages data routing and addressing (e.g., IP addresses).*

> *Layer 4: Transport Layer: Ensures reliable data transfer (e.g., TCP, UDP).*

> *Layer 5: Session Layer: Manages sessions or connections between applications.*

> *Layer 6: Presentation Layer: Translates data formats and encrypts/decrypts data.*

> *Layer 7: Application Layer: Interfaces directly with user applications (e.g., HTTP, FTP).*

> *Understanding How Computers Communicate: The basics of data communication between computers, involving protocols and transmission methods.*

Understanding Physical Network Design: The planning and layout of network hardware and cabling for optimal connectivity.

Understanding Network Cable Topologies: Structures of network cabling configurations:

> *Bus Topology: Single central cable, easy but limited.*

> Star Topology [4.3]: *Devices connected to a central hub, common in LANs.*

> Ring Topology [4.4]: *Devices connected in a loop; each device acts as a repeater.*

> *Mesh Topology: Multiple interconnections for redundancy and reliability.*

Differentiating Network Cable Types: Common network cable types.

> *Coaxial Cable: Shielded cable for high-frequency signals.*

> *Unshielded Twisted-Pair (UTP) Cable: Common for Ethernet networks.*

> *Fiber-Optic Cable: High-speed data transfer using light signals.*

Connecting Network Devices: Different methods to connect devices, including switches, routers, and hubs.

Using Network Services: Essential services for network operation.

> *Domain Name System (DNS): Resolves domain names to IP addresses.*

> Dynamic Host Configuration Protocol (DHCP) [4.5]: *Automatically assigns IP addresses.*

Expanding the Network [4.6]: Approaches to grow network capacity and connectivity options, such as routers and extenders.

> *Using Telephone Circuits: Traditional telephony circuits are used for voice and data transmission in networks.*

> *Network Firewalls: Devices or software that monitor and control incoming and outgoing network traffic for security.*

> *Remote VPN Access: Enables secure remote access to network resources over the internet.*

> *Using Wireless Access Solutions: Technologies like Wi-Fi for enabling wireless network connections.*

> Firewall Protection for Wireless Networks [4.7]: *Using firewalls to secure wireless networks from unauthorized access and threats.*

Remote Dial-Up Access: Legacy technology for accessing networks remotely via telephone lines.

WLAN Transmission Security: Security measures for Wireless Local Area Networks (WLANs) to prevent data breaches.

Achieving 802.11i RSN Wireless Security: Implementing robust security for Wi-Fi networks using the 802.11i standard (e.g., WPA2).

Intrusion Detection Systems (IDS) [4.8]: Systems that monitor network traffic for signs of malicious activity or policy violations.

Summarizing the Various Area Networks: Types of area networks:

LAN – Local Area Network for a limited geographic area.

WAN – Wide Area Network, covering large geographic regions.

MAN – Metropolitan Area Network spans a city or campus.

Using Software as a Service (SaaS): Cloud-based software delivery model:

Advantages: Scalability, cost-efficiency, minimal maintenance.

Disadvantages: Dependency on the internet, limited customization.

Cloud Computing: On-demand access to computing resources (e.g., storage, processing) over the internet.

The Basics of Managing the Network: Fundamentals of network management, including monitoring, troubleshooting, and security.

Automated LAN Cable Tester: A tool for diagnosing LAN cabling issues and verifying cable integrity.

Protocol Analyzers: Devices or software to capture and analyze network packets for troubleshooting.

Remote Monitoring Protocol Version 2: SNMP (Simple Network Management Protocol) version for remote network monitoring and management.

Chapter 05: Information System Lifecycle

Information Systems Life Cycle: Focuses on the stages of an information system from conception to retirement. It includes phases like planning, development, and operation.

Governance in Software Development: Involves ensuring accountability, clear policies, and proper procedures throughout software development, enhancing control and compliance.

Management of Software Quality: Addresses maintaining and improving software quality through testing, reviews, and adherence to standards.

Capability Maturity Model (CMM): A framework that helps organizations improve their software development processes through maturity levels, from initial to optimized.

International Organization for Standardization (ISO): Sets internationally recognized standards for software development, emphasizing quality, safety, and efficiency.

Typical Commercial Records Classification Method: A systematic way to classify and manage business records for easy retrieval and legal compliance.

Overview of the Executive Steering Committee: A high-level group responsible for overseeing major projects, ensuring alignment with business objectives.

Identifying Critical Success Factors: Key elements that must be addressed for a project or business process to succeed.

Using the Scenario Approach: Involves developing various hypothetical situations to explore possible outcomes and prepare for future risks or opportunities.

Aligning Software to Business Needs: Ensures that software solutions are aligned with business strategies and operational goals.

Change Management: A structured approach to transitioning individuals, teams, and organizations to a desired future state, minimizing resistance and ensuring smooth adoption.

Management of the Software Project: The process of planning, organizing, and managing resources to bring about the successful completion of specific software goals.

Choosing an Approach: Selecting the right development methodology (Agile, Waterfall, etc.) based on project size, complexity, and requirements.

Using Traditional Project Management: A linear, structured approach to managing projects, often following the Waterfall model.

Overview of the System Development Life Cycle (SDLC) [5.1]: A framework that outlines the process for creating and maintaining information systems through stages such as planning, analysis, design, and deployment.

Phase 1: Feasibility Study: Initial phase of SDLC where the viability and business value of a proposed system are evaluated.

Phase 2: Requirements Definition: Capturing the detailed specifications of what the system must accomplish, ensuring clarity and completeness for development.

Phase 3: System Design: Translating requirements into detailed architecture and design documents, including system structure, interfaces, and data models.

Phase 4: Development: Involves writing and testing the code, assembling system components, and building the actual product.

Phase 5: Implementation: Deploying the system into production, ensuring it's fully functional and meets the business needs.

Phase 6: Post-implementation: Monitoring and maintaining the system, fixing issues, and making updates as needed after deployment.

Phase 7: Disposal: Safely decommissioning or retiring a system when it's no longer needed, including data migration and archival.

Overview of Data Architecture [5.2]: Defines the structure of an organization's data assets, including storage, management, and integration processes.

Databases: Organized collections of structured data that allow for easy access, management, and updating.

Database Transaction Integrity: Ensures that database operations (transactions) are completed accurately and consistently, following ACID principles (Atomicity, Consistency, Isolation, Durability).

Decision Support Systems (DSS): Tools or systems that help in making informed decisions by analyzing data and presenting actionable insights.

Presenting Decision Support Data: Using dashboards, reports, and other visual tools to effectively communicate DSS outputs.

Using Artificial Intelligence: Incorporating AI technologies to enhance decision-making, automate processes, or predict outcomes.

Program Architecture: The high-level structure of a software application, defining components, relationships, and overall design.

Centralization vs. Decentralization: The debate between managing processes and resources from a single point (centralization) versus distributing them across various units (decentralization).

Electronic Commerce: The buying and selling of goods or services using the internet, including technologies like

online payment systems, secure transactions, and data encryption.

Chapter 06: System Implementation and Operations

Understanding the Nature of IT Services: Overview of IT services, focusing on providing reliable support aligned with business needs.

Performing IT Operations Management: Managing day-to-day IT operations to ensure efficiency and minimize disruptions.

Meeting IT Functional Objectives: Setting and achieving goals that support the organization's IT and business functions.

Using the IT Infrastructure Library (ITIL) [6.1]: Framework for delivering quality IT services, emphasizing service management best practices.

Supporting IT Goals: Aligning IT activities with organizational goals to maximize service value and efficiency.

Understanding Personnel Roles and Responsibilities: Defining clear roles for IT staff to optimize support, management, and security.

Using Metrics: Tracking performance metrics to measure the effectiveness and reliability of IT services.

Evaluating the Help Desk: Assessing help desk performance and its role in providing end-user support.

Performing Service-Level Management: Ensuring that IT services meet agreed-upon levels of performance, availability, and support.

Outsourcing IT Functions: Engaging third-party providers for specific IT services to reduce costs and access expertise.

Performing Capacity Management: Managing resources to meet current and future demands without overextending capabilities.

Using Administrative Protection: Implementing non-technical controls like policies, procedures, and access restrictions to secure IT resources.

Information Security Management: Ensuring confidentiality, integrity, and availability of information through structured security practices.

IT Security Governance: Defining policies, procedures, and responsibilities to govern and control IT security. Assigning roles and responsibilities for managing, accessing, and protecting data.

Data Retention Requirements: Policies for retaining and disposing of data in compliance with legal and business requirements.

Document Physical Access Paths: Recording pathways to physical IT assets for secure access control.

Personnel Management: Hiring, training, and managing IT personnel with a focus on security and operational roles.

Physical Asset Management: Tracking IT hardware and infrastructure to ensure protection and efficient usage.

Compensating Controls: Supplemental controls to mitigate risks when primary controls are insufficient.

Performing Problem Management: Processes to identify and resolve IT problems to prevent recurrence.

Incident Handling: Structured response to IT incidents to minimize impact and restore service quickly.

Digital Forensics: Investigating and analyzing digital evidence for security incidents and legal matters.

Monitoring the Status of Controls: Regularly checking security controls to ensure they function as intended.

System Monitoring: Real-time tracking of system performance and activity to detect issues proactively.

Document Logical Access Paths: Mapping access paths to systems to manage and secure logical access.

System Access and Data File Controls: Mechanisms like passwords, biometrics, and multi-factor authentication to control access. Processes to protect data files from unauthorized access or tampering.

Application Processing Controls: Ensuring the accuracy, completeness, and security of application transactions.

Log Management and Antivirus Software: Collecting, analyzing, and storing logs to track and respond to security incidents. Software to detect, prevent, and remove malware from systems.

Active Content and Mobile Software Code: Managing risks associated with dynamic content (scripts, macros) and mobile software.

Maintenance Controls: Procedures to manage system maintenance, minimizing downtime and preserving security.

Implementing Physical Protection: Safeguarding IT assets through physical barriers, locks, and surveillance.

Data Processing Locations: Security considerations for locations where data is processed or stored.

Environmental Controls: Managing environmental factors (temperature, humidity) in IT areas to protect equipment.

Safe Media Storage: Secure storage practices for physical and digital media to prevent loss or damage.

Chapter 07: Protecting Information Assets

Understanding the Threat: Overview of cybersecurity threats to identify and prepare for potential risks.

Recognizing Types of Threats and Computer Crimes: *Identifying different types of cyber threats, including malware, phishing, and denial-of-service attacks, along with various forms of cybercrime.*

Identifying the Perpetrators: *Types of threat actors such as hackers, insider threats, organized crime groups, and nation-state actors, each with distinct motives and methods.*

Understanding Attack Methods [7.1]: Common attack methods like social engineering, SQL injection, man-in-the-middle, and ransomware, with insights on how each compromises systems.

Implementing Administrative Protection: *Non-technical security measures, including policies, procedures, and training to mitigate human error and enhance security awareness.*

Using Technical Protection: Using technology to defend against threats, including firewalls, intrusion detection systems, and antivirus software.

Technical Control Classification: *Categories of technical controls:*

- **Preventive** – *Block threats before they occur (e.g., access controls).*
- **Detective** – *Identify incidents in progress or after occurrence (e.g., monitoring).*
- **Corrective** – *Mitigate damage and restore functionality post-incident (e.g., backup).*

Application Software Controls: *Controls within software applications to secure data and transactions, such as input validation, output handling, and error management.*

Authentication Methods: *Methods for verifying user identity:*

- **Passwords:** *Most common, though less secure.*
- **Two-Factor Authentication (2FA):** *Combines two methods, like a password and code.*
- **Biometrics:** *Fingerprint or facial recognition for strong authentication.*

Network Access Protection: *Measures to control access to network resources, including VPNs, firewalls, and access control lists (ACLs).*

Encryption Methods [7.1]: Transforming data to protect it from unauthorized access:

- *Symmetric Encryption [7.3] – Uses a single key for encryption/decryption.*
- **Asymmetric Encryption** – *Uses a public-private key pair for secure communication.*

Public-Key Infrastructure (PKI) [7.4]: A framework for managing public-key encryption and digital certificates, essential for secure transactions and communication.

Network Security Protocols: *Protocols to secure data transmission across networks:*

- **SSL/TLS** – *Encrypts web traffic.*
- **IPSec** – *Secures IP communications.*
- **SSH** – *Encrypts terminal access for secure remote logins.*

Telephone Security [7.5]: Protecting telecommunication channels from eavesdropping, caller ID spoofing, and voice phishing attacks.

Technical Security Testing: *Testing methods to assess system security:*

- **Penetration Testing** – *Simulates attacks to find vulnerabilities.*
- **Vulnerability Scanning** – *Scans for known weaknesses in systems.*
- **Code Review** – *Analyzes code to find security flaws.*

Chapter 08: Business Continuity and Disaster Recovery

Debunking the Myths:

Myth 1: Facility Matters – Facilities alone don't ensure business continuity; resilience involves broader aspects.

Myth 2: IT Systems Matter – BC isn't just about IT systems but involves overall organizational preparedness.

From Myth to Reality – Shifting focus from facilities and IT to holistic, strategic continuity planning.

Understanding the Five Conflicting Disciplines Called Business Continuity: Balancing risk management, disaster recovery, emergency response, crisis management, and business resumption.

Defining Disaster Recovery: Focused on restoring IT systems after disruptions to resume normal operations.

Surviving Financial Challenges: Preparing financially for business disruptions, including budgeting for continuity resources and recovery costs.

Valuing Brand Names: Protecting brand reputation by having a solid BC/DR plan that reassures stakeholders and maintains customer trust.

Rebuilding after a Disaster: Strategies to rebuild, both structurally and operationally, after significant disruptions.

Defining the Purpose of Business Continuity: Ensuring critical business functions remain operational during and after an interruption.

Uniting Other Plans with Business Continuity: Integrating emergency response, crisis management, and recovery plans with BC for a unified approach.

Identifying Business Continuity Practices [8.1]: Key practices include risk assessment, business impact analysis, and recovery planning.

Identifying the Management Approach: Adopting a top-down approach with executive support for effective BC program management.

Following a Program Management Approach: Ongoing management of the BC program to adapt to changing risks and organizational needs.

Understanding the Five Phases of a Business Continuity Program:

- *Phase 1: Setting Up the BC Program [8.2]:* Establishing governance, objectives, and resources.
- *Phase 2: The Discovery Process:* Conducting risk assessments and business impact analyses to identify critical areas.
- *Phase 4: Plan Implementation [8.3]:* Developing and implementing actionable plans for continuity.
- *Phase 5: Maintenance and Integration:* Continuously updating and testing the BC plan for alignment with business changes.

Understanding the Auditor's Interests in BC/DR Plans: Auditors focus on evaluating BC/DR plans for compliance, effectiveness, and readiness to minimize operational risks.

Images

Chapter 01: Secrets of a Successful Auditor

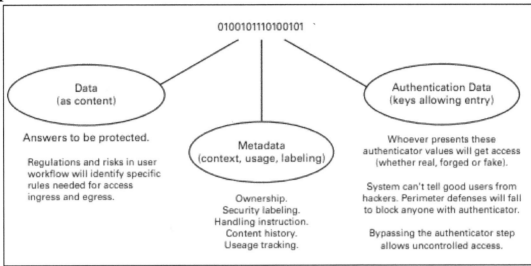

Figure 1.1: Three Types of Data Target Different Uses

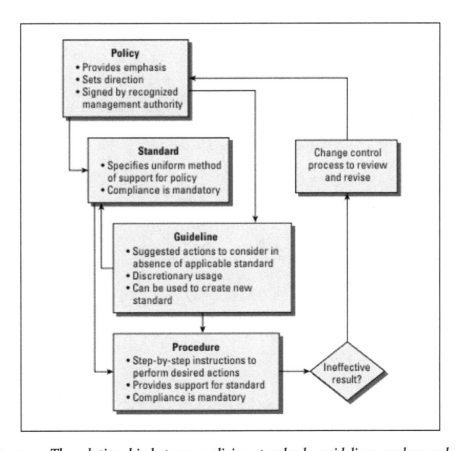

Figure 1.2: The relationship between policies, standards, guidelines, and procedures

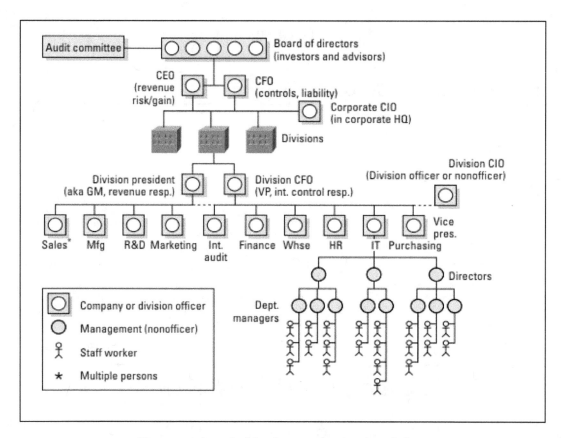

Figure 1.3: A typical business organizational chart

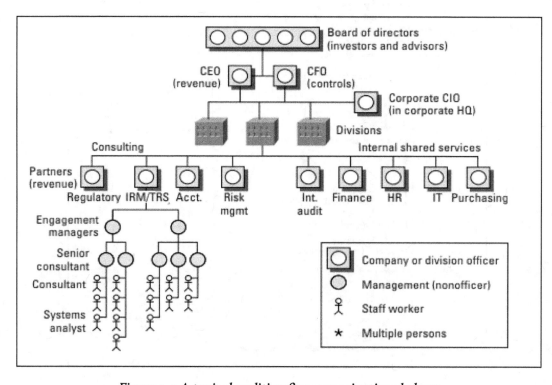

Figure 1.4: A typical auditing firm organizational chart

Chapter 02: Governance

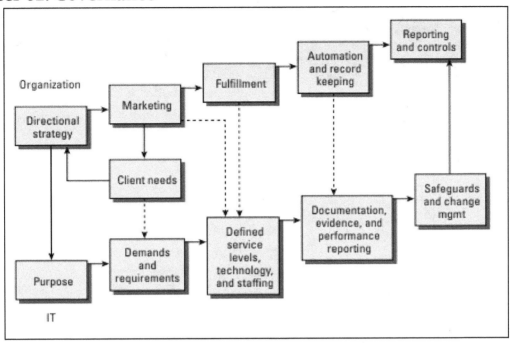

Figure 2.1: IT alignment with organizational objectives

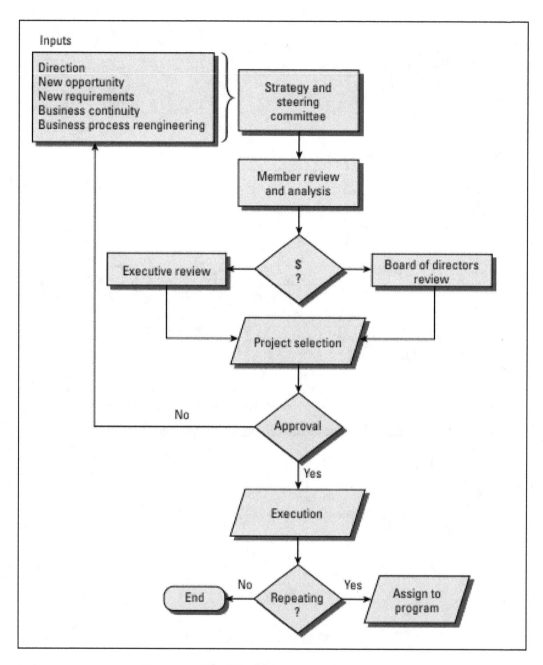

Figure 2.2: The IT steering committee process

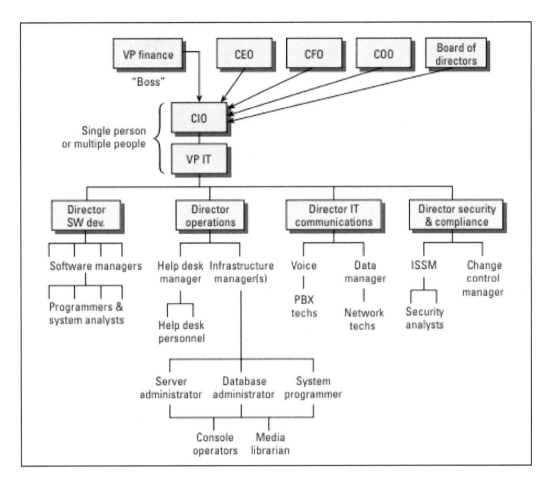

Figure 2.3: Typical IT organizational structure

Chapter 03: Audit Process

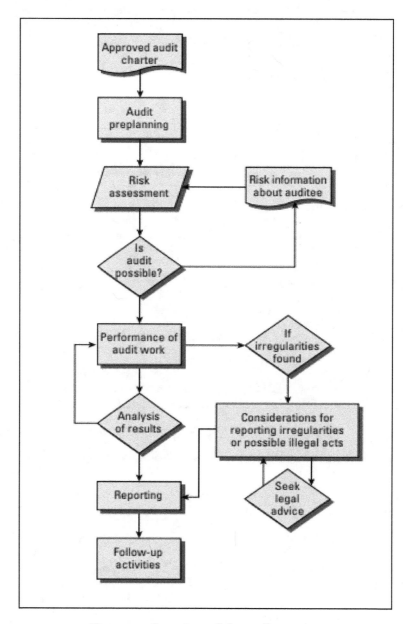

Figure 3.1: Overview of the audit process

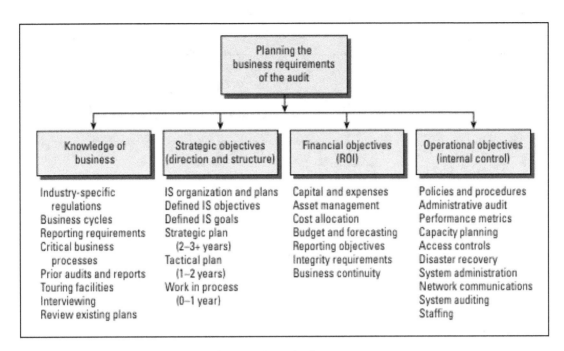

Figure 3.2: Understanding the business requirements

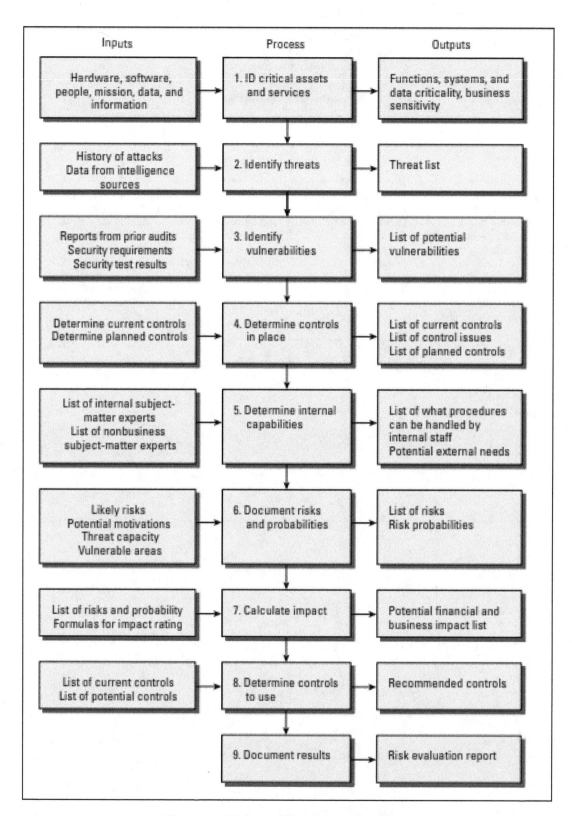

Figure 3.3: Risk analysis process flowchart

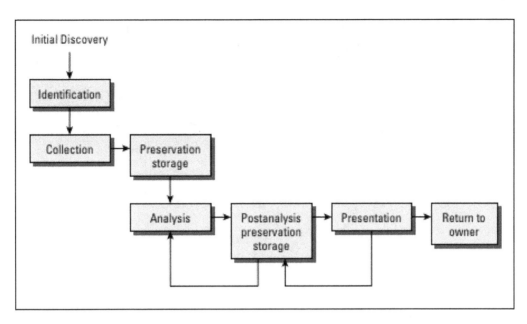

Figure 3.4: The evidence life cycle

Chapter 04: Networking Technology Basic

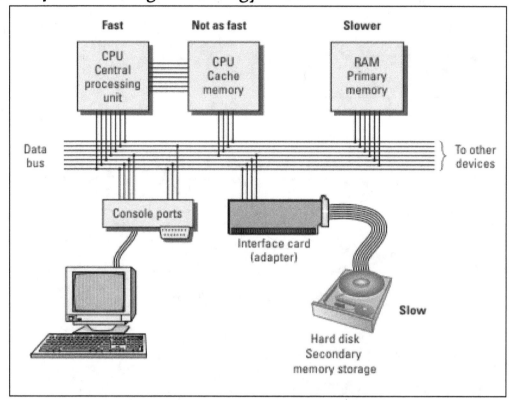

Figure 4.1: Computer hardware architecture

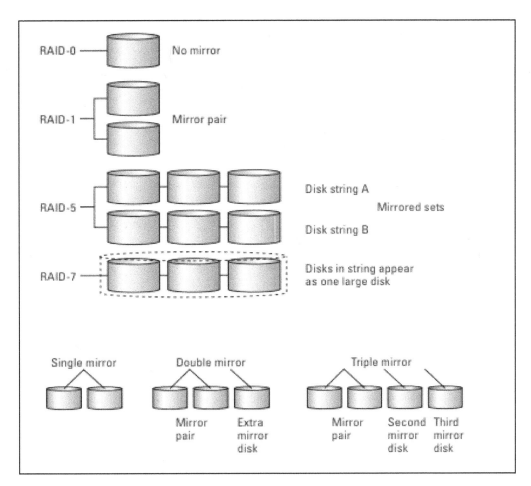

Figure 4.2: Graphical diagram of RAID disk systems

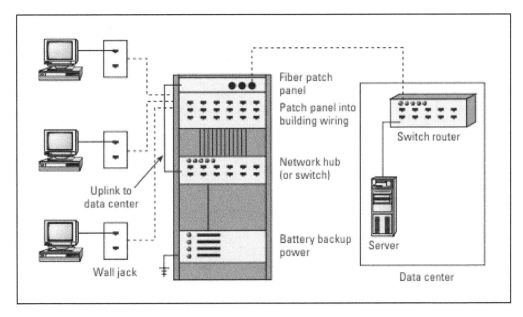

Figure 4.3: Practical application of the star topology

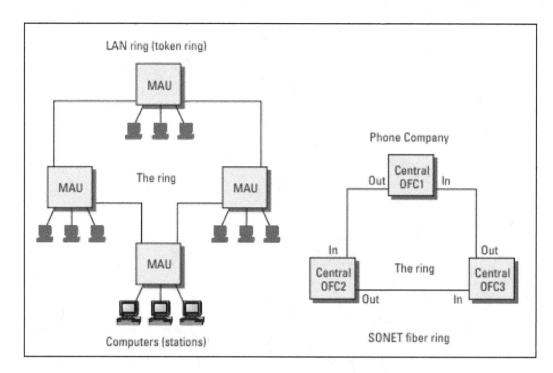

Figure 4.4: Ring topology

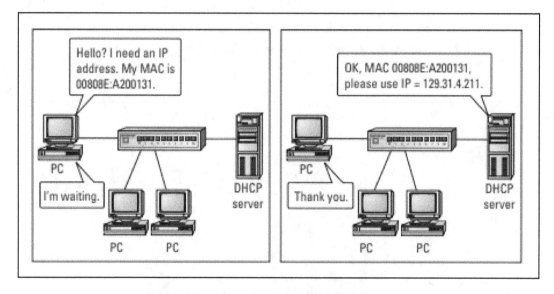

Figure 4.5: How DHCP works

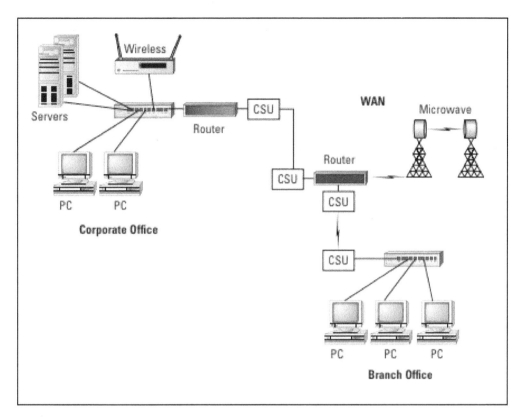

Figure 4.6: Expanding the network

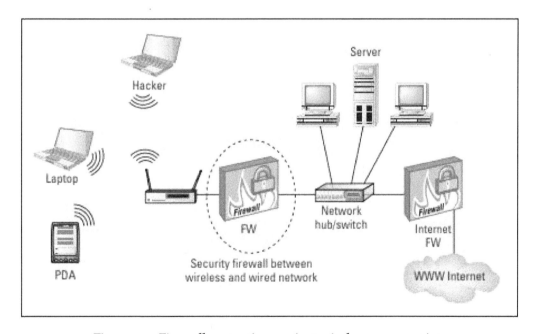

Figure 4.7: Firewall protecting against wireless access points

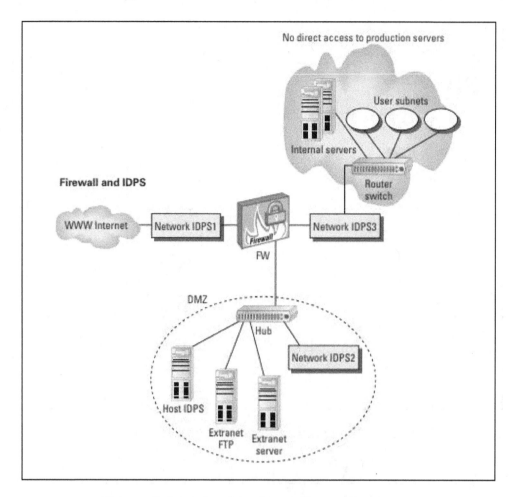

Figure 4.8: Intrusion detection and prevention system

Chapter 05: Information System Lifecycle

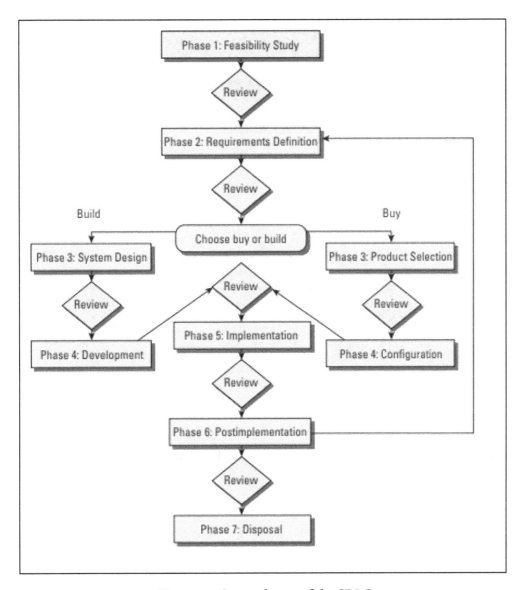

Figure 5.1: Seven phases of the SDLC

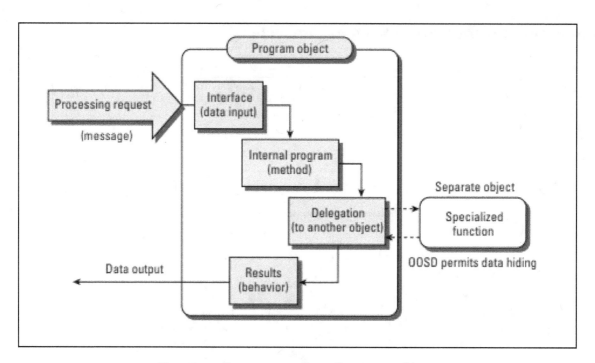

Figure 5.2: Concept overview of program objects

Chapter 06: System Implementation and Operation

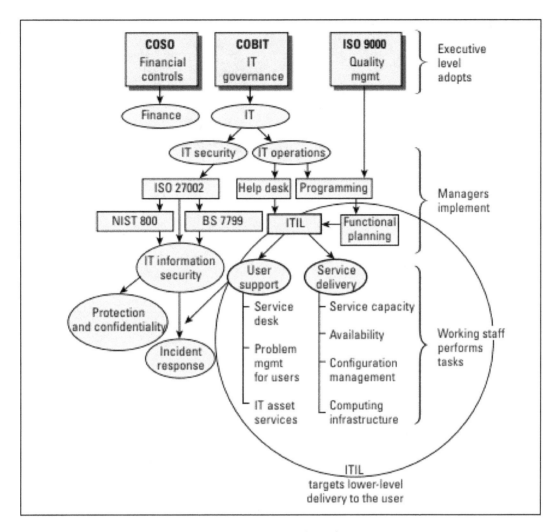

Figure 6.1: Overview of ITIL's purpose

Chapter 07: Protecting Information Assets

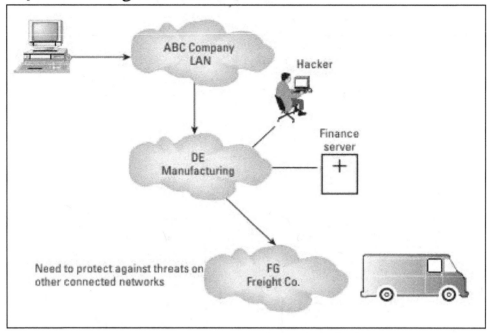

Figure 7.1: Cross-network connectivity

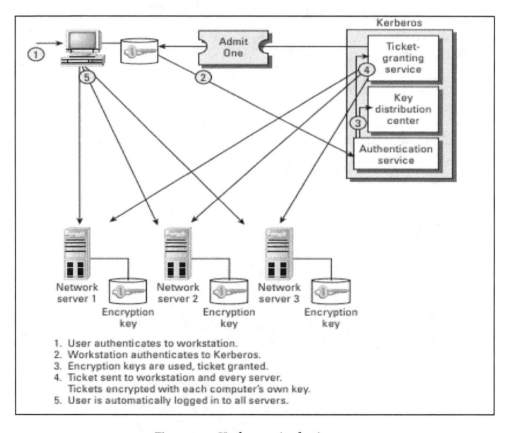

1. User authenticates to workstation.
2. Workstation authenticates to Kerberos.
3. Encryption keys are used, ticket granted.
4. Ticket sent to workstation and every server.
   Tickets encrypted with each computer's own key.
5. User is automatically logged in to all servers.

Figure 7.2: Kerberos single sign-on

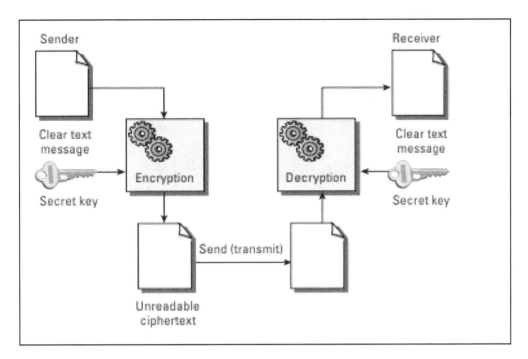

Figure 7.3: Symmetric-key cryptography

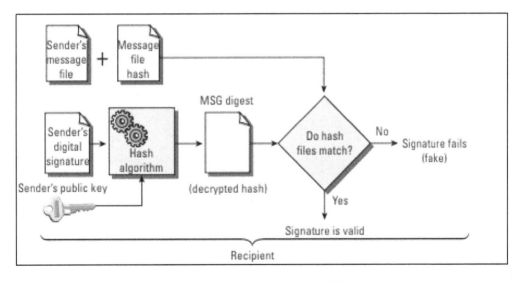

Figure 7.4: Generating a Digital Signature

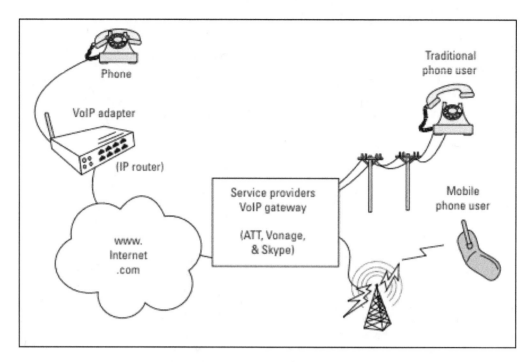

Figure 7.5: Voice over IP network

Chapter 08: Business Continuity and Disaster Recovery

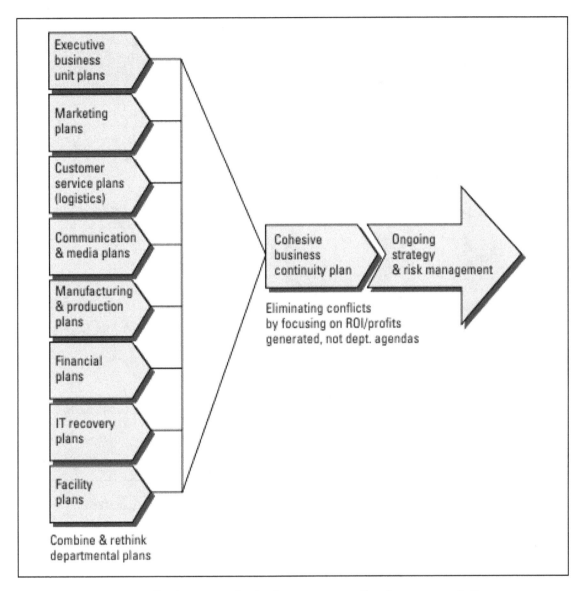

Figure 8.1: Business continuity integrates smaller departmental plans

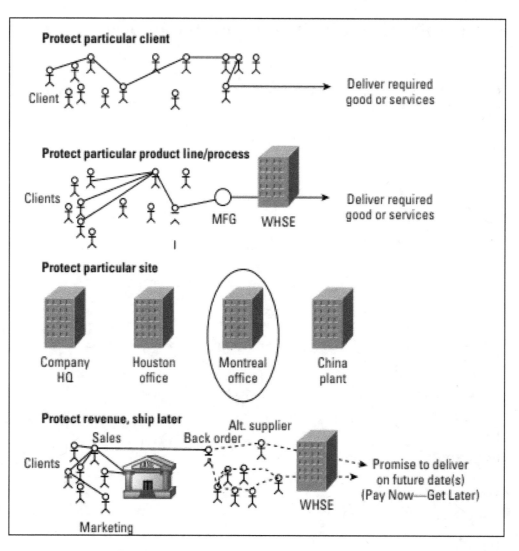

Figure 8.2: Selecting each business process to protect in separate activities

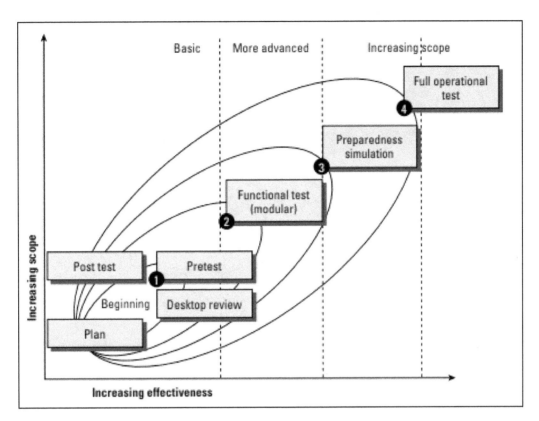

Figure 8.3: The life cycle of testing and exercising the plan